Languages of the World

French

Anita Ganeri

www.raintreepublishers.co.uk
Visit our website to find out more information about Raintree books.

To order:
☎ Phone 0845 6044371
▤ Fax +44 (0) 1865 312263
✉ Email myorders@raintreepublishers.co.uk

Customers from outside the UK please telephone +44 1865 312262

Raintree is an imprint of Capstone Global Library Limited, a company incorporated in England and Wales having its registered office at 7 Pilgrim Street, London, EC4V 6LB – Registered company number: 6695582

Text © Capstone Global Library Limited 2011
First published in hardback in 2011
The moral rights of the proprietor have been asserted.

Edited by Dan Nunn, Rebecca Rissman, and Catherine Veitch
Designed by Marcus Bell
Picture research by Ruth Blair
Originated by Capstone Global Library
Printed and bound in China by South China Printing Company Ltd

ISBN 978 1 4062 2448 1
15 14 13 12 11
10 9 8 7 6 5 4 3 2 1

British Library Cataloguing in Publication Data
Ganeri, Anita
French. -- (Languages of the world)
440-dc22
A full catalogue record for this book is available from the British Library.

Acknowledgements
We would like to thank the following for permission to reproduce photographs: Alamy pp. 5 (© Danita Delimont), 7 (© Penny Tweedie), 8 (© Ancient Art & Architecture Collection Ltd), 21 (© Ken Gillespie Photography), 25 (© Tim Kavanagh / Conceptual); Corbis pp. 13 (© Anna Peisl), 15 (© Hugh Whitaker/cultura), 16 (© Birgid Allig), 20 (© Frank Schnabel), 22 (© Charles Platiau/Reuters); Shutterstock pp. 6 (© Dmitriy Shironosov), 9 (© J.M.P.M. Seijger), 10 (© Andresr), 11 (© Valentyn Volkov), 11 (© ntstudio), 12 (© Ekaterina Pokrovsky), 14 (© Monkey Business Images), 17 (© Monkey Business Images), 18 (© Muriel Pichon), 19 (© Fotomicar), 23 (© Monkey Business Images), 24 (© jackhollingsworthcom, LLC), 26 (© Isabella Pfenninger), 27 (© Nikolay Stefanov Dimitrov), 28 (© ESLINE), 29 (© fcarucci).

Cover photograph of a boy reproduced with permission of Corbis (© Paule Seux/Hemis).

We would like to thank Severine Ribierre for her invaluable help in the preparation of this book.

Every effort has been made to contact copyright holders of material reproduced in this book. Any omissions will be rectified in subsequent printings if notice is given to the publisher.

Disclaimer
All the Internet addresses (URLs) given in this book were valid at the time of going to press. However, due to the dynamic nature of the Internet, some addresses may have changed, or sites may have changed or ceased to exist since publication. While the author and publisher regret any inconvenience this may cause readers, no responsibility for any such changes can be accepted by either the author or the publisher.

Contents

French words are in italics, *like this*. You can find out
how to say them by looking in the pronunciation guide.

French around the world

French is the main language of France. It is spoken in more than 50 countries around the world. It is also spoken in some parts of Canada, Belgium, Switzerland, and Luxembourg.

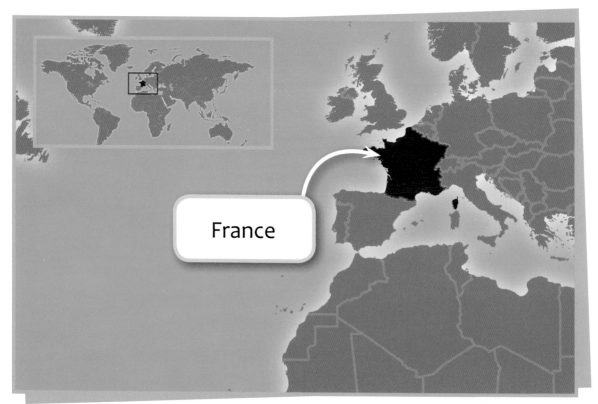

France

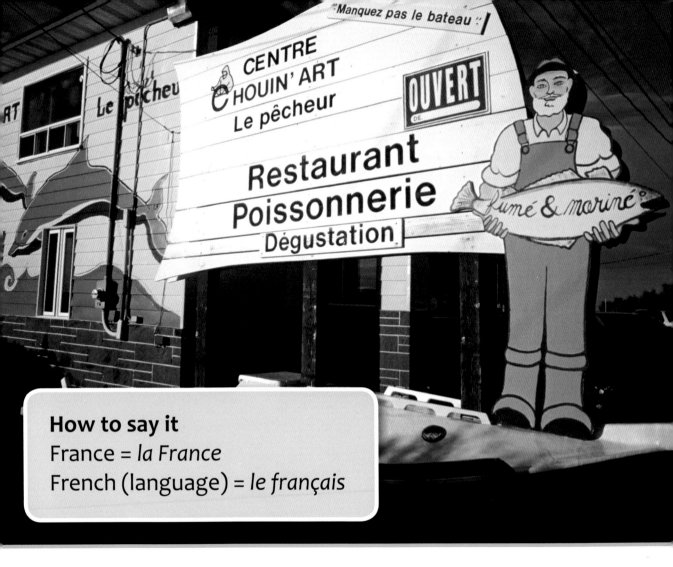

"Manquez pas le bateau"

CENTRE CHOUIN' ART
Le pêcheur

OUVERT

Restaurant
Poissonnerie
Dégustation

fumé & mariné

Le pêcheu

AT

How to say it
France = *la France*
French (language) = *le français*

Millions of people in Africa also speak French. They live in countries that France once ruled. In French, the countries where French is spoken are called *la Francophonie*.

Who speaks French?

About 140 million people speak French as their first, main language. About 190 million more speak French as their second language.

Chatting to friends is a good way to practise speaking French.

Many people speak French in Africa.

French may sound very different when it is spoken outside France. People say words in a different way. They also use words borrowed from other languages.

French and English

French is called a "Romance" language. This is because it comes from Latin. Latin was the language spoken by the Romans. English does not come from Latin. English is not a Romance language.

Some old buildings have Latin writing.

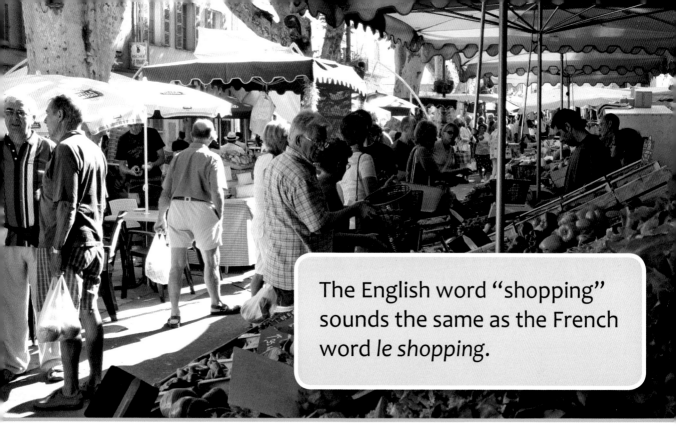

The English word "shopping" sounds the same as the French word *le shopping*.

Some French words are used in English, such as *café* and *ballet*. Some English words are used in French, such as *le shopping* and *le week-end*. Can you guess what the words in the box below mean?

la banane   *le chocolat*   *la famille*   *la plante*
(See page 32 for answers.)

Learning French

French uses the same alphabet as English but some letters are said differently. The best way to learn French is to listen to how French people speak and try to copy them.

How to say it
yes = *oui*
no = *non*
thank you = *merci*

Words that name things are called nouns. In French, nouns are feminine or masculine. If a noun is feminine, the word for "the" is *la*. If a noun is masculine, the word for "the" is *le*.

Saying hello and goodbye

Friends and family usually kiss each other several times on the cheek when they meet. They may say "*Salut!*" People say "*Bonjour!*" or "*Bonsoir!*" to be more polite.

How to say it
Hello (to friends) = *Salut!*
Good day/morning = *Bonjour!*
Good evening = *Bonsoir!*

Salut can mean "goodbye" as well as "hello". There are different ways of saying "See you again". People say "*Au revoir!*" or "*A bientôt!*" *Bonne nuit* means "goodnight".

Talking about yourself

To tell someone your name you say
"*Je m'appelle …*" ("My name is …").
To tell them how old you are, you say
"*J'ai [huit] ans*" ("I am [eight] years old").

How to say it
My name is … = *Je m'appelle …*
I am … years old = *J'ai … ans*

How to say it
I come from ... = *Je viens de ...*
I speak ... = *Je parle ...*

To tell someone where you come from you say "*Je viens de ...*" ("I come from ..."). If they ask you if you speak French you can say, "*Oui, je parle français!*" ("Yes, I speak French!").

Asking about others

To ask someone what their name is you say "*Comment tu t'appelles?*" "*Quel âge as-tu?*" means "How old are you?"

How to say it
What is your name? = *Comment tu t'appelles?*
How old are you? = *Quel âge as-tu?*

How to say it
Where do you live? = *Où habites-tu?*
    or *Où habitez-vous?* (polite)
Do you speak English? = *Parles-tu
    anglais?* or *Parlez-vous anglais?*

To find out where someone lives you can
ask "*Où habites-tu?*" To ask if they speak
English you can ask "*Parles-tu anglais?*"
If you are talking to someone older use
vous instead of *tu* to be polite.

17

At home

Homes in countries where people speak French can be very different. In cities people often live in apartments or flats. Some apartment buildings are new, but many are very old.

How to say it
house = *la maison*
flat = *l'appartement*

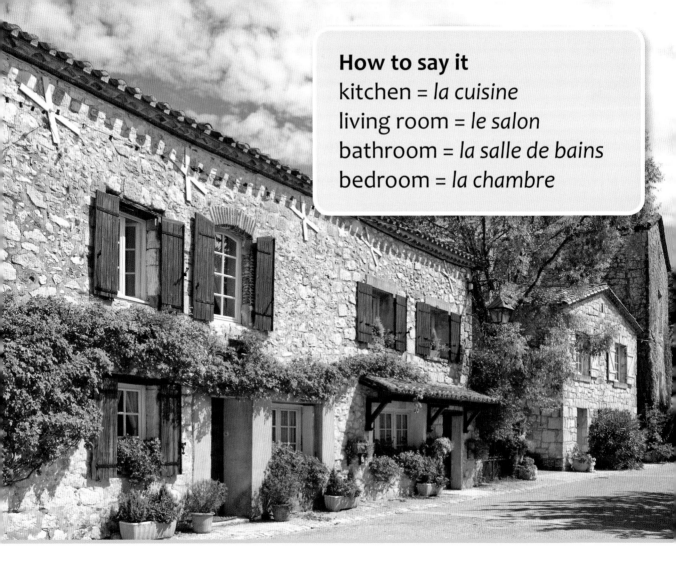

How to say it
kitchen = *la cuisine*
living room = *le salon*
bathroom = *la salle de bains*
bedroom = *la chambre*

In the countryside people usually live
in houses. Some are large and old, like
this one. Others are modern. Some large
country houses are called *châteaux*,
which means "castles".

Family life

Families in the countries where people speak French can be large or small. In some places, children, parents, and grandparents all live together in the same home.

How to say it
mother = *la mère*
father = *le père*
brother = *le frère*
sister = *la soeur*

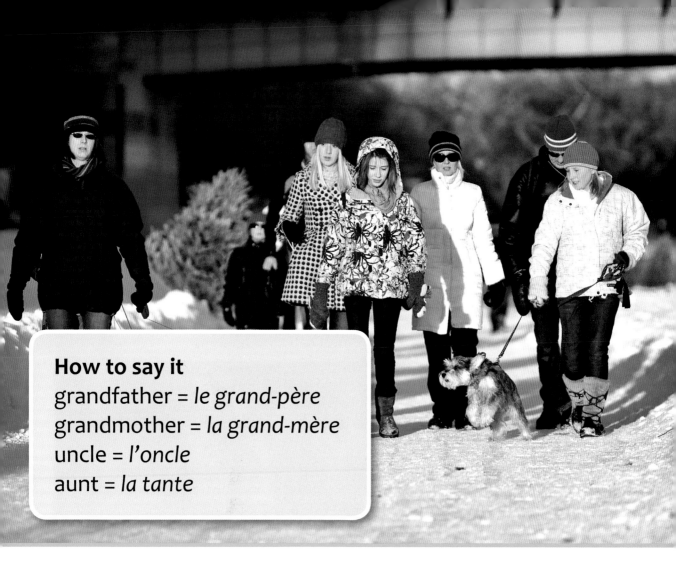

How to say it
grandfather = *le grand-père*
grandmother = *la grand-mère*
uncle = *l'oncle*
aunt = *la tante*

The French word for "family" is *la famille*.
This family is out for a winter walk in
Canada. They are taking their dogs with
them. The French word for "dogs" is
les chiens.

At school

In France children go to primary school from the ages of 6 to 11. Then they go to a middle school until they are 15 years old. They go to high school from age 15 to 18.

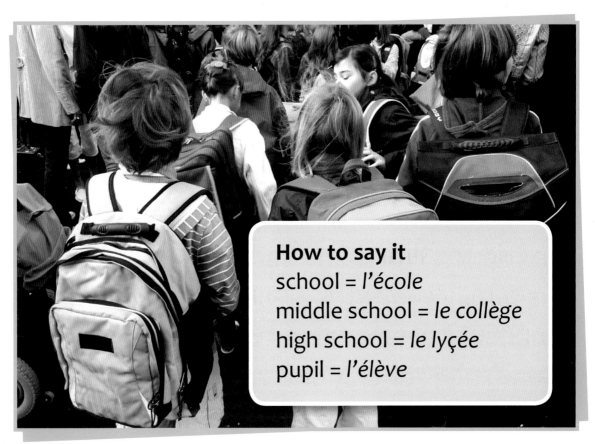

How to say it
school = *l'école*
middle school = *le collège*
high school = *le lyçée*
pupil = *l'élève*

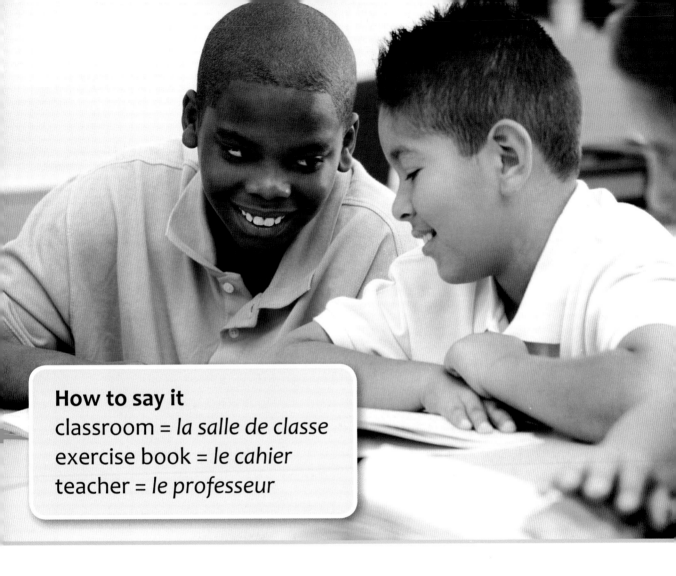

How to say it
classroom = *la salle de classe*
exercise book = *le cahier*
teacher = *le professeur*

At school children learn many different subjects, including French. Children in countries that do not speak French may also learn French at school.

Having fun

People in French-speaking countries like doing many different things in their spare time. They listen to music, go to the cinema, and enjoy going to cafés.

How to say it
music = *la musique*
cinema = *le cinéma*
café = *le café*

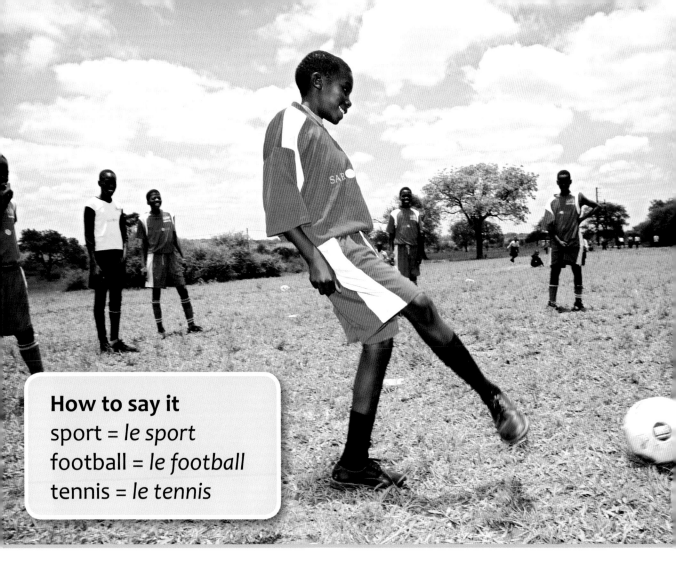

How to say it
sport = *le sport*
football = *le football*
tennis = *le tennis*

In many French-speaking countries football is popular. People in France also like cycling, tennis, and playing *pétanque*, which is a type of bowls.

Food

French food is famous all over the world. In France, people like to eat long loaves of bread called *baguettes*. These are freshly baked every morning.

How to say it
bread = *le pain*
fruit = *les fruits*
vegetables = *les légumes*

How to say it
cheese = *le fromage*
paté = *le pâté*
I'm hungry = *J'ai faim*
Enjoy your meal! = *Bon appétit!*

Lots of different kinds of cheese are eaten in France. The French word for "cheese" is *le fromage*. *Paté*, which is made from meat, is also popular.

Clothes

What clothes do you like wearing? Most people who live in French-speaking countries probably wear the same sort of clothes as you! In French the word for "clothes" is *les vêtements.*

How to say it
clothes = *les vêtements*
jeans = *le jean*
T-shirt = *le tee-shirt*
jumper = *le pull-over*

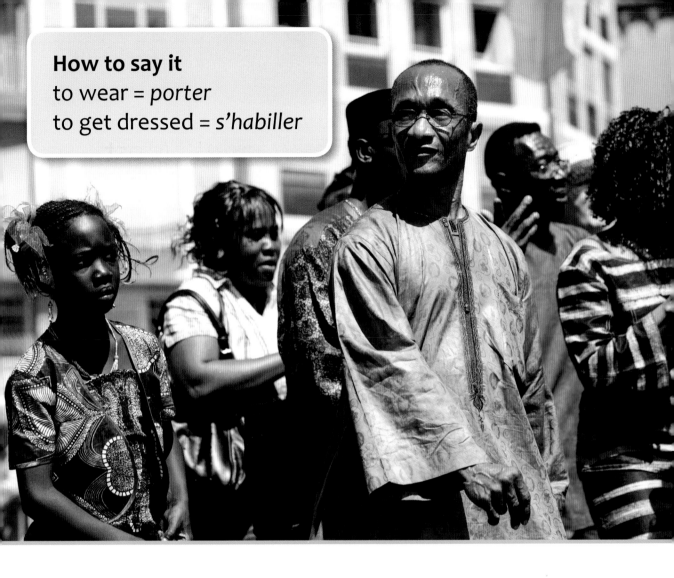

How to say it
to wear = *porter*
to get dressed = *s'habiller*

In some French-speaking countries in Africa people wear brightly coloured robes. You may see African people in France wearing these clothes, too.

Pronunciation guide

English	French	Pronunciation
apartment (flat)	l'appartement	lapartemon
aunt	la tante	la taant
bathroom	la salle de bains	la sal de ban
bedroom	la chambre	la shambr
bread	le pain	le pan
brother	le frère	le frair
café	le café	le cafay
cheese	le fromage	le fromaaj
cinema	le cinéma	le seenayma
classroom	la salle de classe	la sal de klass
clothes	les vêtements	lay vaytmon
Do you speak English?	Parles-tu anglais?	Paarl too onglay?
Enjoy your meal!	Bon appétit!	Bon appaytee
exercise book	le cahier	le kayay
father	le père	le pair
football	le football	le footbal
fruit	les fruits	lay frwee
get dressed (to)	s'habiller	sabeeyay
goodbye	au revoir!	oh revwar
good day/morning	bonjour!	bonjoor
good evening	bonsoir!	bonswoir
goodnight	bonne nuit!	bon nwee
grandfather	le grand-père	le gronpair
grandmother	la grand-mère	la gronmair
hello	salut!	saloo
high school	le lycée	le leesay

house	la maison	la mayzon
How old are you?	Quel âge as-tu?	Kel aaj a too?
I am … years old	J'ai … ans	Jay … on
I come from …	Je viens de …	Je veean de …
I'm hungry	J'ai faim	Jay fan
I speak …	Je parle…	Je paarl
jeans	le jean	le jeen
jumper	le pull-over	le pewl-over
kitchen	la cuisine	la kweezeen
mother	la mère	la mair
music	la musique	la mewzeek
My name is …	Je m'appelle…	Je mappel
no	non	non
paté	le pâté	le patay
pupil	l'élève	laylev
school	l'école	laykol
See you soon	A bientôt!	A beeyanto
sister	la soeur	la sir
sitting room	le salon	le sallon
sport	le sport	le spor
teacher	le professeur	le profaysir
tennis	le tennis	le tayniece
thank you	merci	mairsee
the	le (m); la (f)	le; la
T-shirt	le tee-shirt	le teeshirt
uncle	l'oncle	lonkl
vegetables	les légumes	lay laygewm
wear (to)	porter	portay
What is your name?	Comment tu t'appelles?	Common too tappel?
Where do you live?	Où habites-tu?	Oo abeet too?
yes	oui	wee

Find out more

Books

50 French Phrases, Susan Martineau (b small publishing, 2009)
First French Words, Neil Morris (Oxford University Press, 2007)
French is Fun with Serge, the Cheeky Monkey!, Sue Finnie
(dvd activity pack: BBC Active, 2006)

Websites

kids.nationalgeographic.com/kids/places/find/france
www.bbc.co.uk/schools/primaryfrench/

Index

Meaning of the words on page 8

la banane = banana
le chocolat = chocolate

la famille = family
la plante = plant
